This journal is also a companion for the writing
and reflection prompts offered in the book:

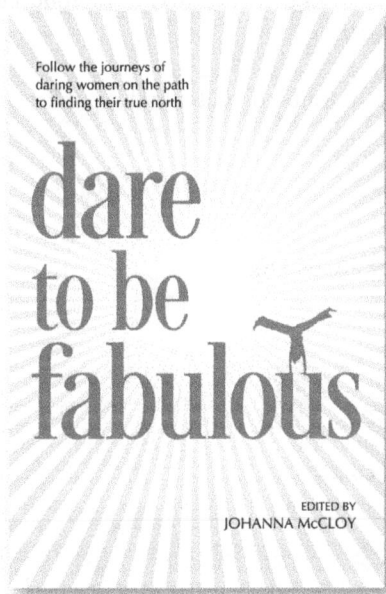

Follow the journeys of
daring women on the path
to finding their true north

dare
to be
fabulous

EDITED BY
JOHANNA McCLOY

Dare to be Fabulous:
Follow the journeys of daring women
on the path to finding their true north

Edited by Johanna McCloy

© 2022 Bordertown Publishing

A list of the sources for all featured quotes in this publication is available at daretobefabulous.com

ISBN 978-0-9975963-4-2

Printed in the United States of America

Bordertown
Publishing

Berkeley, CA
bordertownpublishing.com

Track the path to your own true north.

"A sheltered life can be a daring life as well.
For all serious daring starts from within."

~ Eudora Welty

"I'm not funny. What I am is brave."

~ Lucille Ball

"It is good to have an end to journey towards;
but it is the journey that matters in the end."

~ Ursula K. Le Guin

"You've been criticizing yourself for years and it hasn't worked. Try approving of yourself and see what happens."

~ Louise Hay

"She found joy and wonder in every little thing.
And joy and wonder always found her."

~ Katrina Mayer

"I'd rather regret the risks that didn't work out than the chances I didn't take at all."

~ Simone Biles

"The most courageous act is still
to think for yourself. Aloud."

~ Coco Chanel

"Follow your passion. Stay true to yourself.
Never follow someone else's path unless you're
in the woods and you're lost and you see a path.
By all means, you should follow that."

~ Ellen DeGeneres

"A bird doesn't sing because it has an answer,
it sings because it has a song."

~ Joan Walsh Anglund

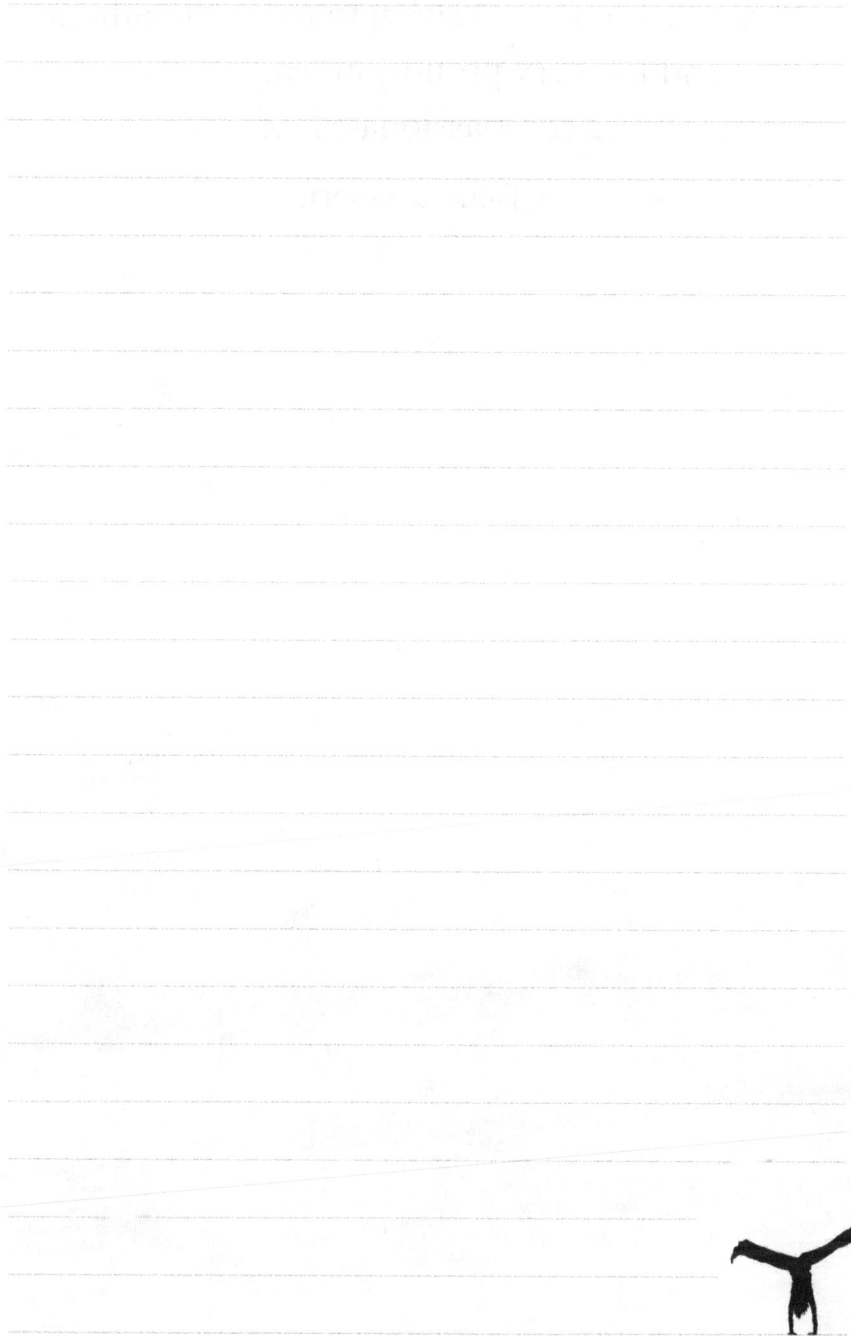

"It takes courage and strength to be empathetic,
and I'm very proudly an empathetic
and compassionate leader."

~ Jacinda Ardern

"The trouble with the rat race is that even if you win, you're still a rat."

~ Lily Tomlin

"Remember no one can make you
feel inferior without your consent."

~ Eleanor Roosevelt

"I look forward to growing old
and wise and audacious."

~ Glenda Jackson

"Mother Teresa didn't walk around complaining about her thighs – she had shit to do."

~ Sarah Silverman

"On this sacred path of Radical Acceptance,
rather than striving for perfection,
we discover how to love ourselves into wholeness."

~ Tara Brach

"In art and dream may you proceed with abandon.
In life may you proceed with balance and stealth."

~ Patti Smith

"The one thing I do not want to be called is First Lady. It sounds like a saddle horse."

~ Jacqueline Kennedy Onassis

"A champion is defined not by their wins, but by how they can recover when they fall."

~ Serena Williams

"He who laughs, lasts."

~ Mary Pettibone Poole

"Women may be the one group
that grows more radical with age."

~ Gloria Steinem

"Life is creation.
Self and circumstances the raw material."

~ Dorothy M. Richardson

"Compassion practice is daring. It involves learning to relax and allow ourselves to move gently toward what scares us. The trick to doing this is to stay with emotional distress without tightening into aversion, to let fear soften us rather than harden into resistance."

~ Pema Chödrön

"People said, "Jane, forget about this nonsense with Africa. Dream about things you can achieve.""

~ Jane Goodall

"I have bursts of being a lady,
but it doesn't last long."

~ Shelley Winters

"It is the sweet simple things in life
which are the real ones after all."

~ Laura Ingalls Wilder

"I'm not going to limit myself just because people won't accept the fact that I can do something else."

~ Dolly Parton

"Security is mostly a superstition. It does not exist in nature, nor do the children of men as a whole experience it. Avoiding danger is no safer in the long run than outright exposure. Life is either a daring adventure, or nothing."

~ Helen Keller

"'What is courage?' I ask. 'Bearing witness.
That is a form of courage.'"

~ Jessica Stern

"Can't nobody fly with all that shit. Wanna fly, you got to give up the shit that weighs you down."

~ Toni Morrison

"To love ourselves and support each other
in the process of becoming real is perhaps
the greatest single act of daring greatly."

~ Brené Brown

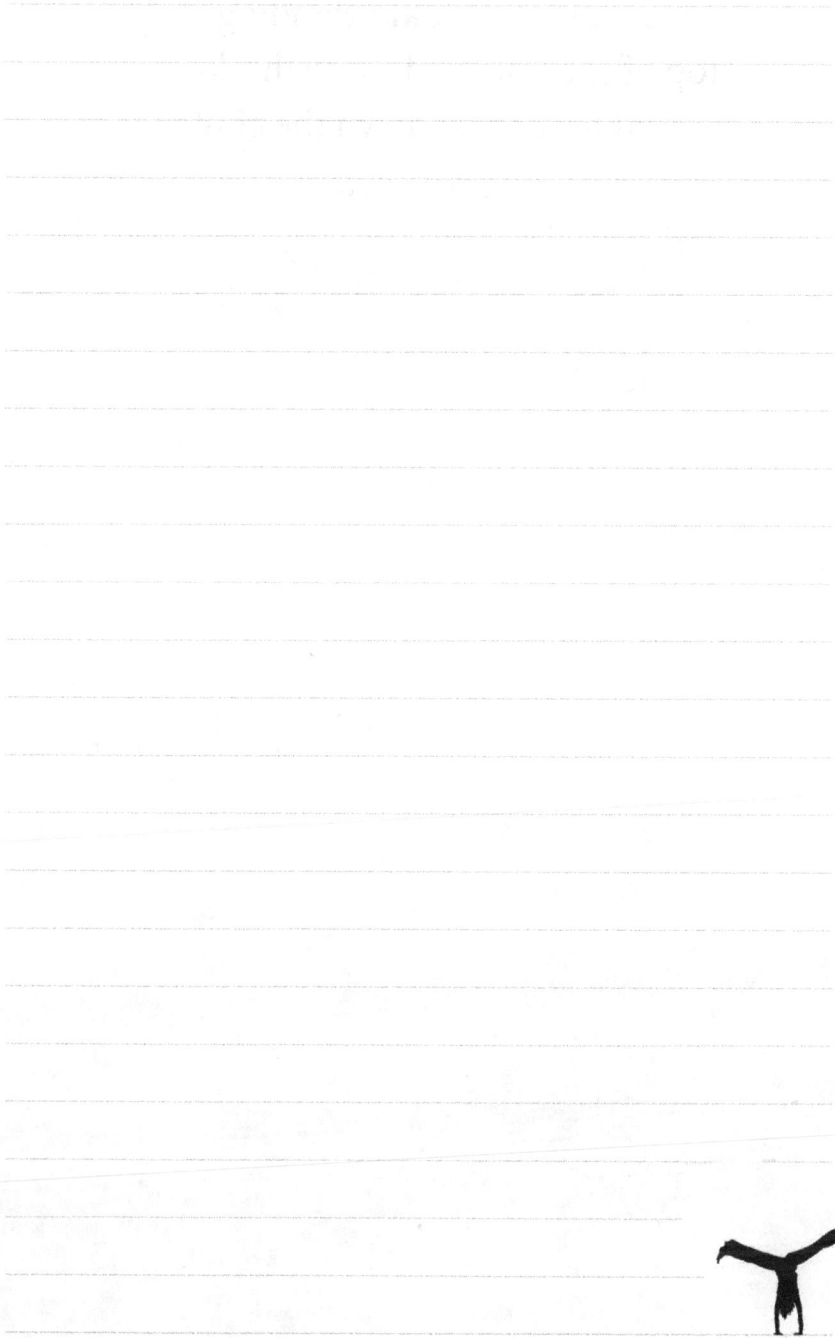

"You can't be that kid standing at the top of the waterslide, overthinking it. You have to go down the chute."

~ Tina Fey

"You can't shake hands with a clenched fist."

~ Indira Gandhi

"Life is about not knowing, having to change, taking the moment and making the best of it, without knowing what's going to happen next. Delicious ambiguity."

~ Gilda Radner

"'Why the fuck not me?' should be your motto."

~ Mindy Kaling

"I believe that every single event in life happens
in an opportunity to choose love over fear."

~ Oprah Winfrey

"I am not afraid of storms,
for I am learning to sail my ship."

~ Louisa May Alcott

"Always be a first-rate version of yourself,
instead of a second-rate version of somebody else."

~ Judy Garland

"Smile in the mirror. Do that every morning, and you'll start to see a big difference in your life."

~ Yoko Ono

"I, for one, am certainly going to continue to raise a little hell."

~ Doris "Granny D" Haddock

"Ego says, "Once everything falls into place, I'll feel peace. Spirit says, "Find your peace, and then everything will fall into place.""

~ Marianne Williamson

"I am an endangered species / But I sing no victim's song / I am a woman I am an artist / And I know where my voice belongs / I know where my soul belongs / I know where I belong."

~ Dianne Reeves

"Life shrinks or expands in
proportion to one's courage."

~ Anais Nin

"Your opponent, in the end, is never really the player on the other side of the net, or the swimmer in the next lane, or the team on the other side of the field, or even the bar you must high-jump. Your opponent is yourself, your negative internal voices, your level of determination."

~ Grace Lichtenstein

"Why should we all dress after the same fashion?
The frost never paints my windows twice alike."

~ Lydia Maria Child

"Don't be distracted by emotions like anger, envy, resentment. These just zap energy and waste time."

~ Ruth Bader Ginsburg

"Act boldly and unseen
forces will come to your aid."

~ Dorothea Brande

"My life has been long, and believing that life loves the liver of it, I have dared to try many things, sometimes trembling, but daring still."

~ Maya Angelou

"Well-behaved women seldom make history."

~ Laurel Thatcher Ulrich

"You may be disappointed if you fail,
but you are doomed if you don't try."

~ Beverly Sills

"Much love to everyone
who is busy being a blessing."

~ Germany Kent

"Another belief of mine: that everyone else my age is an adult, whereas I am merely in disguise."

~ Margaret Atwood

"Courage can't see around corners,
but goes around them anyway."

~ Mignon McLaughlin

"In our ordinariness we are most bizarre."

~ Ntozake Shange

"Life is a verb, not a noun."

~ Charlotte Perkins-Gilman

"You become courageous by doing courageous acts . . . Courage is a habit."

~ Mary Daly

"Perfectionism is the voice of the oppressor."

~ Anne Lamott

"It's your outlook on life that counts. If you take yourself lightly and don't take yourself too seriously, pretty soon you can find the humor in our everyday lives. And sometimes it can be a lifesaver."

~ Betty White

"Freshness trembles beneath the surface of Everyday, a joy perpetual to all who catch its opal lights beneath the dust of habit."

~ Freya Stark

www.ingramcontent.com/pod-product-compliance
Lightning Source LLC
Chambersburg PA
CBHW051901090426
42811CB00003B/419